THE WELLBEING ACTIVITY BOOK

Published by Sourcebooks
P.O. Box 4410, Naperville, Illinois 60567-4410
(630) 961-3900
sourcebooks.com

Originally published in 2022 in the United Kingdom by Michael O'Mara Books Limited.

Printed and bound in China.
OGP 10 9 8 7 6 5 4 3 2 1

THE WELLBEING ACTIVITY BOOK

Self-Care Activities Through the Seasons

Amy Birch
Illustrated by Kat Kalindi

sourcebooks

Introduction

It makes sense that taking care of yourself ought to be a priority. After all, when you're feeling better, everything else in life tends to flow better too. The irony is that in the demanding tumult of the everyday, that simple equation so often gets forgotten. We plow on as best we can without the chance to pause to think whether there might be another way. But the good news is that even the smallest things add up and make a difference to your wellbeing. Just making that decision to care about yourself enough to try can be the start of an important shift. Small changes, acts of kindness, and support towards yourself build into a new experience of life that feels just that bit more balanced, more meaningful, more compassionate, more flexible, more creative, more reflective, and more joyous—or, to keep it simple, generally nicer.

There are lots of different ways that you can support your wellbeing, and the activities in this book offer simple, creative ideas to make the most of that variety. Some are designed to dial down anxiety and stress levels; some aim to bring more happiness, purpose, or connection to your life; while others work to hook you up to your own power to make positive changes. They are organized into spring, summer, autumn, and winter—because the seasons have always had a powerful effect on our mood and the way we go about

our daily lives. As temperatures rise and fall, and weather and light levels tempt us outdoors or drive us inside, our lives adjust in response, meaning each new season brings with it fresh opportunities to support our wellbeing.

That said, if you prefer, you can flick through this book and find the activity that feels like the right fit for right now. You know what might make a difference to your day better than anyone. And, of course, some of the ideas here might not be for you—we're all different and at different points—but,

equally, maybe you're looking to challenge yourself. No single activity or exercise has the power to completely transform your life. There is no magic formula for contentment, but that doesn't mean we can't aim to make things a bit better. And sometimes all we need is some inspiration to get started.

So care for yourself as a good friend would, and see what a difference prioritizing your wellbeing can make.

SPRING

The New

Spring is all about new life. The temperature starts to
rise, and we witness a burst of activity and growth.
See if you can channel that springtime energy
by trying something completely new. It doesn't
matter what it is. The point is to experience that
sensation of novelty and discovery, and maybe even
a bit of adventure. That means reaching for the next
episode in a much-loved series isn't going to cut
it—although it absolutely has its own kind of value
(turn to "The Familiar" on page 156 for more).

It can be daunting to try something new.
We can find ourselves feeling like we have to be
'good' at it straight away. But the reality is that

when we start something new, we are learners. We are not supposed to be good at it. When we see a child try something new for the first time, we aren't disappointed or critical of them when they don't exhibit the skill of an expert. We expect them to have a go, break things, not get it right. If you try a new walk, you might get lost; if you try a new sport, you might score the odd touchdown, and your first knitted creation is going to be uneven and full of holes. And that is how it should be.

Take the pressure off, leave the judgment at the door, enjoy being a learner again, and see if you can give yourself permission to simply enjoy experiencing something new. You might never do it again; it might not be for you—that's the point: you don't know until you try. But maybe you'll find something that you want to come back to. And just like that, your world's a bit bigger.

Stop Multitasking

You've only got one head and two hands. Trying to do multiple things at once means we're not giving our full attention to any one thing, and it can be stressful switching from task to task. It's also energy-sapping for our brain, which makes it an ineffective and inefficient means of getting things done.

Even when you feel like the weight of tasks is closing in on you, the best thing you can do is approach them one at a time. Choose what needs your attention right now, and just do that. Only start on something new when you're finished with the last task. Give each thing your full focus.

If you find your mind whirring with all the other things that you feel you have to do, try writing them down. Having a list not only transfers all those to-dos from your mind to paper; it means that you can see the extent of what needs doing—it might be long, but there is an end to it! It can also help you to prioritize and put your tasks in order.

This one sounds super simple, but when we're in that frenetic, sped-up headspace, slowing down can be the last thing we want to do. So the first task on your list might be taking a break for five minutes to stand outside and breathe some fresh air, or making a cup of tea. You'll then be in a more relaxed headspace to tackle what needs doing.

That Bit Better

What would make your day just that bit better? Perhaps it would be finishing work on time, calling a friend, watching your favorite TV show, or taking the slightly longer route home through the park so you can see the spring flowers.

We can be so focused on just getting through the day, caught up in the momentum of mentally checking things off and adding to our to-do list, that we forget to pause and remember that we can choose to do things differently, even if that's just adding an extra dash of brightness to an otherwise standard day.

It only takes a couple of minutes in the morning to ask yourself the question and come up with an answer. Of course, the key is remembering to do it—that to-do list momentum can be pretty powerful. One of the most reliable ways is to associate it with a daily habit. For instance, you could link it to your morning shower or when you're sipping your coffee or when you're sitting on the bus. That way you have built in a daily reminder to ask: "What would improve my day today?"

Aim for something small and achievable so that even if you're feeling stressed and rushed, you can reassure yourself that it won't disrupt the flow of your day too much.

What's great about this activity is that it's not only a gesture of care towards yourself; it also doubles up as a small act of empowerment as you actively choose to do something that's just for you.

Wonder

What blows your mind? The magnitude of the universe, the composition of an opera, the way trees can talk to one another? Whatever it is, why not spend some time reveling in that sensation. That might mean getting wrapped up in your subject—for example, watch a documentary, read a book, or research online to learn more. Or it might mean a more relaxed approach. Perhaps the joy is in the mystery. In which case, you could just lean back and allow that feeling of wonder to percolate through your body.

Think about how you might engage with that feeling of wonder through your senses. For instance, by watching a sunset, listening to a piece of music without any distractions, or taking a walk through the woods. Enjoy letting the extraordinary in.

Digital Spring-Clean

For many of us, our devices are our constant companions. We turn to them for work, for fun, when we're bored, and when we're lonely. We use them to interact with the people in our lives as well as the wider world. As a result, they have the potential to influence us a great deal, sometimes negatively. If you've noticed you're spending too much time online or staring at your smartphone, it might be time to try this exercise.

The first step in a digital spring-clean is observation. That means paying attention to the various ways in which your device affects you, whether that's helping you to feel connected or hounded by distractions. Think about the way in which your devices impact your behavior, thoughts, and mood. The next step is to decide what changes you'd like to make, which mainly means creating boundaries. Our devices are like a doorway, and it's up to us to decide who and what we open the door to. Then, it's time to:

17

Blitz your apps

Uninstall the ones you don't use regularly
(you can always install them again if you
find that you need them), or tidy them into
an archive folder if you aren't sure.

Social media

This can be a biggie so give it some time.
Consider each of the platforms you use and how
they affect your life. Think about how you use
them, who you follow, and what you post. What
value do each of these elements add to your
life? How might you experiment with change?

Work vs. personal

Are there any boundaries that you'd like to
try with this? For instance, do you need to
have work email on your personal phone?

Notifications

Consider which notifications you actually need
(be honest), and then silence the rest.

Unsubscribe

Streamline your inbox by searching for the word
"unsubscribe." This will bring up all mail that
you receive that you can unsubscribe from.

Switch off

Do you ever turn off your phone?
Would you like to?

Are there any other ways in which you use
your devices that you'd like to change?

Meditate

An oldie but a goodie, meditation is included in lots of wellbeing advice for a very good reason. It offers a way of quieting the mind, detaching it from thoughts, worries, and distractions, in order to experience what it's like to be simply conscious. The practice can help us feel relaxed, help with anxiety regulation, and lower stress levels, among other benefits.

Of course, not many of us can imagine sitting for hours with a perfectly tranquil and empty mind. The good news is that you don't have to. There are many different forms of meditation, and you can find one that feels like a fit for you. It's also worth keeping in mind that meditation is a skill, and like all skills, you have to start small and build up through practice.

Try this simple breathing-based meditation to give you a sense of what it can be like.

1. Sit in a comfortable position.
   This can be on a chair or on the floor.

2. Take a moment to feel settled.

3. Close your eyes, or drop and soften your gaze.

4. Allow yourself to breathe naturally.

5. Bring your attention to your breath. As you inhale and exhale, notice how it feels: allow your attention to move through your chest, shoulders, and belly. Notice the sensation of the air moving through your nose.

6. If your mind wanders—and it will—just gently guide it back to your breath.

7. Keep this up for two or three minutes. With more practice you can slowly lengthen the time.

8. If you'd like to go further, there are many meditation apps that can help you get started, as well as videos on YouTube and other online tutorials, or you could join a meditation class.

Mindfulness Practice

Mindfulness is one of those popular forms of meditation that you might have already come across. When we practice mindfulness, we are paying full attention to the present moment with an attitude of acceptance, compassion, and curiosity. Day to day, we often don't notice that our minds are busy with worries about the future or memories of the past. Mindfulness reconnects us with the present through our bodies and the sensations we experience. It is also a way in which we can observe our thoughts and feelings at more of a distance, without getting caught up in them. Regular practice can have a significant positive impact on our health and wellbeing.

There are lots of mindfulness-based activities in this book, including "Body Scan," "Grounding," "Bake Yourself a Cookies," and "Go for a Walk in the Rain." There are also some great apps and videos online that will help you build your practice.

To get a feel for it, have a go at the following mindful meditation next time you're out on a walk.

1. Loosely clasp your hands in front of you so your attention is fully on your legs and feet.

2. Soften and drop your gaze towards the ground.

3. As you step forward, pay attention to how the swing of your leg feels, then how it feels when your heel meets the ground and your weight transfers forward onto your toes.

4. Notice how the other leg swings forward to meet it.

5. Continue to walk forward at a slow, leisurely pace while keeping your attention on your legs and feet as they move.

6. When your mind wanders—and it will—just gently guide it back to the sensation of walking.

7. Keep this up for a couple of minutes.

Don't worry when you realize you're thinking about other things. You're not doing anything wrong. In fact, that's the very core of mindfulness: this process of our mind wandering away before we gently guide it back to the present.

Eye-Spy Beauty

Next time you're traveling somewhere, keep an eye out for
beauty. This is a great one to do in spring as the natural
world offers up so many options. It might be something
obvious like a tree in full blossom or a striking wall mural,
or it might be more subtle, like the reflection of a streetlight
in a puddle or the symmetry between two buildings.
Look at the big picture as well as the small, such as
the skyline of a city and the iridescence of a beetle.

And don't forget that there is beauty to be found outside
of the purely visual: the songs of birds, the regular rhythm
of a train, the scent of damp leaves, or cooking aromas
wafting from a restaurant can all contain beauty.

Sometimes you'll be able to appreciate beauty as you go,
but at other times, you'll need to pause and absorb. It can
be helpful to keep this intention in mind and allow yourself
a bit of extra time so you don't feel you have to rush on.

Feel the Music

One of the ways that we connect to music is through our emotions. We often ascribe emotions or a story to individual pieces, and listening to music can have a profound effect on our mood. We instinctively select music that mirrors our emotional state or sets the tone for how we'd like to feel.

However, we can often forget to deliberately tap into this powerful potential. Much of the time, music is more of

an accompaniment than a focus, providing a background
soundtrack to all sorts of activities: cooking, socializing,
studying, crafting, driving… And there's nothing wrong with
that, but it can mean that we overlook the rich experience that
comes when we focus on and really listen to the music itself.

Think about the music that you love. What might you like
to give your attention to right now? And if you can't right
now, how about later? How would you like to experience
it? And what about live music: concerts, festivals? Do you
play an instrument or sing? Or would you like to learn?
There are many ways to connect to music. Audience,
performer, dancer, composer: what might you like to try?

Keep a Two-Week Diary

There are lots of great reasons to keep a diary, but one of the lesser-used ones is to check in with what you actually spend your days doing. It's a good way of turning off autopilot and taking a fully conscious approach to the way you're currently living your life and how you might benefit from making changes.

While you can keep the diary in digital format if you prefer, loose sheets of paper tend to be better as once you're finished, you can spread out the diary in front of you and get an immediate sense of how your daily habits and patterns play out across the weeks.

To create the template for your diary, divide
one piece of paper into seven columns,
representing the seven days of the week, then
draw twenty-four lines in each column, correlating
with the twenty-four hours in each day. Do this
again so you have one for each week of your
two-week diary. Now you just have to start filling
it in. Remember to choose pretty typical weeks.

In order to be as accurate as possible, it's best to fill it in
at the end of each day, or if you find it tricky to remember
the details, you could set reminders on your phone so you
only have to fill in a few hours at a time. It may seem like
a hassle, but remember, it's just for a couple of weeks.

Start by shading in those hours during which you were asleep. Then, for all the other hours, note down what you were actually doing. You can choose the level of detail and what to particularly focus on—for instance, it might be illuminating to keep a note of every time you take a break (or don't take a break) while working. Color-coding particular types of activities can also be helpful to quickly assess how you weight your time.

Be as honest as possible. Noting that you went to bed at 10:30 p.m. when in reality that was just the start of an hour-and-a-half-long process of brushing teeth, replying to messages, and watching a few YouTube videos before eventually turning the light off at midnight, means that you miss out on the opportunity to reflect on how the process impacts your wellbeing.

When you have a couple of weeks filled in, lay out the diary in front of you. Does anything immediately strike you? Do you get enough sleep? Is there a big gap between meals where you maybe feel grumpy or sluggish? Is there enough fun stuff, active stuff, social stuff? How much screen time do you have? Is there anything missing?

❀

Remember, there's no right or wrong way to live your life, but by consciously paying attention to how you spend the hours of your day, you can better understand how your daily habits impact your mood and quality of life.

❀

If you do decide to make changes, you could consider continuing the diary for a few weeks to help you stay committed and track the difference.

31

Make Marks on Paper

…of anything you like and with anything you like. Lifelike realism, expressionistic daubs of color, doodling, blueprints for a spaceship—it doesn't matter what style or subject matter you go for. This is all about the process. You're not necessarily creating art; you're just creating. And you don't have to be 'good' at it—in fact, being 'good' is most definitely not the point. But if you find that you enjoy it, perhaps you could do it more.

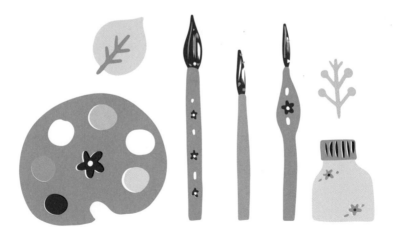

Organize and Minimize

There's no better way of welcoming in spring than with a good clear-out. Whether your intention is to declutter or just to organize what you've got, the process can be a deeply satisfying one. The key, however, is to keep it manageable. Consider the time and energy that you've got and what's achievable—you don't want your bed covered with clothes when it's time to sleep.

The precise process will depend on what you're organizing, but here are some useful general principles to follow.

1. Remove everything and give the area a good clean.

2. Sort your possessions into categories. It might be as simple as "keep" and "donate," or perhaps more specific piles relating to where you're going to store them, for example. Don't be afraid to have a "for later" pile. Some decisions require a little more time.

3. Now that you know what you've got and the space is clean and clear, you can consider whether you might like to organize things differently than before. Perhaps those kitchen utensils might be better closer to the stove, or you only need a few pairs of shoes within easy reach and the rest can be stored elsewhere.

4. When you're finished putting everything away again, don't forget to take a few minutes to admire your handiwork.

5. When it's time to turn to the "for later" pile, allow yourself to connect with any emotions that come up. After all, if something is in this pile, then there's something tricky about the decision of what to do with it.

6. Before you give your "donate" pile to charity, sort through it in case there are any good candidates for upcycling (see the next page).

Upcycle

Clothes, furniture, garden tools, books…nearly any object can, with the right perspective, be given a new lease on life with upcycling. There are important wellbeing pay offs to upcycling as well, such as using your hands, creativity, and enjoying the satisfaction of completion. It also involves a transformative experience, where new value is bestowed onto an object that might otherwise be dismissed as old, broken, or useless. Rigid ideas about what something is or should be used for are replaced with a more flexible, imaginative approach. Not a bad mindset to cultivate.

Think about skills you already have and could put to use, as well as skills you're keen to learn. Perhaps this is the excuse you've been looking for to try your hand at something like upholstering, carpentry, or metalwork. Or there are many crafting and DIY skills that aren't so ambitious and can be learned via online tutorials. However, a lot of upcycling doesn't need any specialist knowledge or equipment at all. You can always base your projects around what you have at hand. Nor do you always have to make extensive changes to have an impact. Switching out buttons on a shirt or handles on a chest of drawers, for example, instantly turns the mundane into the bespoke. Consider what difference a change of color, use, effect, or decoration might have.

Upcycled items can also make great gifts, so could that old thingamiwhatsit be revamped for someone else?

Feed Your Curiosity

Feeding your curiosity is a great antidote to
doomscrolling Twitter or listlessly bingeing Netflix.
For some of us, learning is associated with school,
curriculums, and assessment. We learned in order
to be tested and graded, and that was about it.
No wonder we can find ourselves leaving it behind
or sticking with familiar subjects where we feel
comfortable and secure. The learner mindset can also
get left behind, replaced with a sense that if we aren't
already proficient in an area, then it's not for us.

But what about all those questions that you've
pondered over the years and never had an answer to?
Such as: How do records translate vinyl grooves into

complex audio? What is it actually like on Mars? How does the internet work? Why do leaves turn orange in autumn? Perhaps you caught a headline or a snatch of conversation that piqued your curiosity, but you never came back to it. Or maybe there are wider subjects that you'd like to understand more about, such as quantum physics or the history of a particular period.

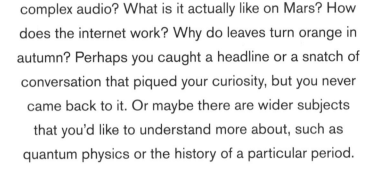

Why not set a goal to discover a bit more? The scope is totally up to you. You could start small with a bit of googling, perhaps a few YouTube videos, escalating to a documentary or an article or two. Or you could always try a bookshop (online or in person). Start browsing, select a book that appeals to you, and read the first few pages. What do you think? Would you like to know more? Don't worry if it's not for you. No one's watching, and there won't be any tests.

Check In with What Really Matters

The more we are able to live in step with our values, the greater our sense of wellbeing. It can help boost self-esteem, confidence, and our sense of fulfillment and purpose. Having our values clear in our minds also helps us to navigate our way through life.

What are your values? You might never have consciously named them, before but you'll likely have an idea of what they are. Think about qualities or principles that inspire you personally. Try writing them down to help you gain clarity. It's important

to keep in mind that these are your values and
yours alone. Sometimes we can feel we ought to
have certain values because of what society or our
family says. Make sure that each value you write
on your list feels like it matters to you deeply.

Are there any decisions or conflicts that you're currently
facing? How might your values help guide you?

Refresh a Room

*This can be a good one to do after
"Organize and Minimize" on page 33.*

Your environment can play an important role in your mood
but that doesn't mean you have to embark on a full interior
makeover to enjoy a boost. Rearranging furniture costs
nothing and can bring new life into a room. It might seem
superficial, but the impact is not only in changing the
way a space looks; it also comes from exercising your
power to make changes and explore new perspectives.

The first step in refreshing a room is to think about how
you use it. Has anything bugged you in the past, such as
bad lighting or not having a surface within easy reach to
put down your cup? Perhaps you regularly knock your shin
against the coffee table because it's too close to the sofa.

Move the big pieces first, such as sofas, beds, tables, and so on (take care moving heavy or awkward pieces —only do what feels comfortable), so you have the foundations sorted. Don't be afraid to pull furniture away from walls or even take things away—sometimes decluttering furniture is the key to making a room feel more spacious. You could also consider swapping pieces of furniture with other rooms. If you've got treasures squirreled away, could they be put on display?

Finally, don't forget about lighting. Placing lights at different levels can really transform a space and make it feel warmer and more inviting. If you've got a floor or table lamp, try it in different spots to see the effect.

Bring an experimental mindset to your room refresh. You can always try it out for a little while and put it back again if it doesn't work out.

Forest Bathing

Forest bathing is the practice of slowing down and immersing yourself in nature. It was first developed in the 1980s in Japan, where it's called *shinrin-yoku.* Studies suggest that just two hours of time spent mindfully in a forest can help reduce blood pressure, lower the stress hormone cortisol, and improve concentration and memory.

Leave your phone and camera behind if you can, and allow your senses to guide you. You're not trying to get anywhere while forest bathing, rather fully embracing and connecting with the peaceful environment around you.

Look at the different shapes, colors, and movements.

Listen for birdsong, the rustling of leaves, the creak of branches, and your footsteps in the leaf litter.

Breathe deeply and inhale the aromatic phytoncides that plants give off, which boost the human immune system.

Taste the air as it passes through your mouth into your lungs.

Place your hands on the trunks of trees or pick up leaves, blossom, twigs, and seed casings to feel the detail.

Forest bathing was, as the name suggests, developed with forests in mind, but you can use the same principles in any natural environment. And while the original studies examined the effect of two hours surrounded by nature, much shorter periods are still beneficial. So even if you've only got ten minutes in your local park, it's definitely still worth it.

Plan a Day Off

That means a proper day off, leaving all your usual responsibilities at the door. So, no work or productive pursuits. A day off is about fun, not what you can get done. This isn't like those weekends when you finally paint the bathroom or file your tax return or sort through your wardrobe; this is about leisure.

What would you like to do? Where would you like to go? What would you like to eat? Who would you like to see? Start planning. Not too rigidly but enough so you aren't left pondering what to do on the day—a sure fire way of slipping into that to-do list or slumping in front of Netflix (nothing wrong with that of course, but only if it's part of the plan). Next, decide on a date and make sure you can stick to it. Give yourself permission to embrace the break and engage fully with the activities you've chosen.

If a whole day seems too hard to commit to, or you'll have to wait a long time for it, how about half a day? If even that feels tough given your daily responsibilities, it might take more time and planning to arrange. But if it feels like giving yourself a day off will do you good, don't give up!

Seasonal Chef

See if you can create a meal that only uses seasonal ingredients—that's fruit, veggies, and other products that are grown and available locally. You can do this at any time of year, but late spring and early summer bring some especially delicious produce to enjoy. What's available will depend on where you live in the world, so find out what's at its best near you now. Your local greengrocer or market, if you've got one, are often a good source of information. You could even search out a seasonal

food calendar—there are lots of free ones online. Print it out and attach it to your fridge for a regular reminder of what to look out for when you shop.

Eating produce in season ensures that you're getting it at its most nutritious and tastiest. If you've ever tried a strawberry out of season, you'll already know the difference. By using seasonal produce, you're also cutting down your carbon footprint—it hasn't been shipped around the world, nor has energy been expended to force plants to grow out of season. And you're also supporting local growers. What's not to like?

SUMMER

Take It Outdoors

Perfect for those warm, sunny days of summer, this one's super simple: Whatever you're doing, could you take it outside? Studying, reading, working, snacking, scrolling through Twitter… can you do the same thing, but outdoors?

You'll need a comfortable, shady spot. Perhaps a well-positioned bench in a local park, or if there's a nearby patch of grass, you could always bring a blanket and cushion and stretch out.

Just by changing settings, we expand our world, and by being outside, we get the added benefits of sunlight (see "Sunshine" on page 153 for more), fresh air, nature, and community.

Celebrate

We're used to celebrating birthdays and seasonal, cultural, and religious festivals, but is there anything that's more personal to you that you feel deserves celebrating? It might be a yearly anniversary or a one-off. How you celebrate is up to you, whether it's a huge party with everyone invited or a private, precious ritual; the point is to pause and honor the important things in life. Thinking about what you'd like to celebrate can also be a chance to check in with your personal values (look back to "Check In with What Really Matters" on page 40 for more).

And, as ever, don't forget the little things either. Whether it's a piece of work that went well or a first step towards a new goal, make sure it doesn't go unnoticed. You don't have to pop the champagne and set off fireworks; just simply allow the feelings—whether of pride, satisfaction, relief, joy, or anything else that crops up—all the way in. Recognize your achievement and the part you played in it. Give yourself that pat on the back. You know what it means to you.

Tiny Worlds

Take a break from the busyness and
cares of your own world by immersing
yourself in a totally different one.

Find a patch of grass and lie down—you can put a
blanket and cushion down first if you want to make
it more comfortable. Keep still so as not to scare
away what might be living there and see what you
can spy. Don't worry about identifying your finds; this
activity is more about observation than categorization.
Think about the lives you're watching, what they
spend their days doing, what their priorities are, how
they negotiate their habitat. Consider the different
scales of life that exist around you and how they
intermingle without you even being aware of it.

Trees are another great source of exploration. One oak tree, for instance, can be home to over 2,300 different species—and that's not including all the different fungi and micro organisms that thrive among its roots and branches. The undersides of leaves and the crevices in bark can be rich treasure troves of life, especially in summer.

If you don't fancy getting up close to creepy-crawlies, you could limit your hunting to plant life. Even a simple, unassuming patch of scrub can be home to a surprisingly diverse variety of species. In fact, to take it even further, something as seemingly barren as a paving slab can be home to lichens, and even a lamppost may house mosses and algae.

Achievable Goal

If you're feeling stuck, just getting one thing done can help start to shake you free from the inertia. It gives you the opportunity to experience a small buzz of completion. Breaking down big goals into bite-sized tasks can help us avoid feeling overwhelmed as well as establish a sense of momentum. For instance, maybe you can't get that essay finished today, but you can write a paragraph. You can also use this principle to tackle that annoying thing on your to-do list that just never gets done or to credit yourself for an everyday task that you don't normally celebrate achieving.

The key with this one is to make sure that the one thing you do is genuinely achievable. Being overly ambitious can be counterproductive, as it sets us up for failure and disappointment, which in turn means we're less likely to try it again. One way to do this is by setting some boundaries. Give yourself a time limit—depending on your task it could be thirty minutes, a couple of hours, an afternoon, or a day, but not longer, and usually the shorter the better. Use your self-knowledge to inform what's going to work for you. For instance, if you know that you don't suit focusing for long periods of time, keep it brief. You could even set a timer to help you. Equally, if you know that you tend to err on the side of optimism, take this into account and deliberately set your target lower. If it's longer than an hour, schedule in breaks. Give these breaks a time limit too. Once you have set your boundaries, stick to them.

When you've finished the task, pause to check in with what the experience was like for you and how it feels to have finished. Give yourself credit for doing it (see "Celebrate" on page 53). If you didn't finish the task, give yourself the benefit of a debrief, and ask yourself what got in the way. Try to avoid self-blame, and instead exercise your curiosity. What might have helped? Was the goal actually that bit too ambitious? Could you break it down into even smaller chunks? Did it bring up strong emotions? Might it help to talk these through with someone? Perhaps the task is something that you feel you ought to want to do but in fact isn't for you? This way, not only will you be able to tailor the exercise better next time, you'll also know a little bit more about yourself.

Grow Herbs

Growing your own herb garden brings all sorts of wellbeing benefits. For instance, watching the plants develop and mature can be a helpful reminder of change and growth when you're feeling stuck or stagnant. Caring for them with regular watering, potting on, fertilizing, and so on can make for a nurturing and grounding routine. Even getting it wrong and perhaps losing a plant can offer us a chance to practice failure (see "Get Good at Failure" on page 116).

Of course, this applies to caring for any sort of plant, but herbs are special. They can be used as a great start to a mindful break. Take a leaf or sprig, crush it between your fingers, and inhale the intense fragrance of the oils. When you use your homegrown herbs in your cooking, remember to give your full attention to that first taste and see if you can identify the flavors that your very own herbs have bestowed.

Choose any herbs that you like and will thrive in the conditions that you have. Grow them from seed or buy them as plants. If you don't have space outdoors, many will grow happily indoors with sufficient care and a big enough pot.

Body Scan

The body scan is a simple but effective mindfulness technique that helps you to release tension held within your body. Move your attention slowly through your body, noticing any sensations you encounter along the way, such as pain, tightness, warmth, or tension. As you do this, allow each part to relax before moving on. You can do this exercise anywhere, but it's useful to first practice when you're in a quiet place where you won't be disturbed. That way, you'll find it easier to use in less familiar or more distracting environments.

1. Sit (or lie) in a comfortable position, and begin to lengthen and deepen your breaths.

★

2. Place your attention in your toes. Are you aware of any sensations?

★

3. If you notice tension, pause and, while breathing deeply, allow that part to relax. Imagine the tension leaving your body with your breath and disappearing into the air.

★

4. Repeat this process through the rest of your body, working upwards into your feet, calves, knees, thighs, bottom, back, shoulders, upper arms, elbows, lower arms, palms, fingers, neck, jaw, face, eyes, and scalp.

5. Once you reach your scalp, start to move your attention back down your body in the opposite order, ending with your feet.

★

6. When you reach your feet, notice how they feel on the floor. Stay with that feeling for as long as you want before getting up.

★

7. If you don't have time to do a full scan, you could use a condensed version instead where you focus on the parts of your body where you can already detect tension. It's also a great practice to do before bed as it can help your body and mind to deeply relax.

Blue Therapy

The power of nature isn't limited to green spaces—blue spaces are known to have their own distinct restorative properties. Studies have shown that the sound of water and the quality of light as it plays upon its surface have a relaxing effect on us, and the color blue itself is associated with a sense of calm and peacefulness. Most of us will recognize that feeling when we first catch sight of the sea, but the power of blue extends to much smaller bodies of water too: lakes, rivers, streams, waterfalls, ponds…they all count. Even a fountain can help bring about this effect.

Think now about where your own local sources of blue are. You could also consider what activities you enjoy doing in the water. Swimming, surfing, and boating all bring you into contact with water and offer the additional benefits of physical activity.

Soothing Solitude

Do you get enough quality me-time? We're used to the idea of making quality time with family and even friends, but how about with ourselves? It's easy to forget that we all have a relationship with ourselves, the nature of which shows up in how we think and feel about ourselves and how we talk to and treat ourselves. And just like with any other relationship, there are things we can do to develop a strong and supportive one.

Going for a walk, taking a bath, meditating, singing nineties pop classics while cooking, cozying up on the sofa with a good book—what do you enjoy doing in your own company? Even if you live alone, it's worth considering whether you're getting enough *quality* time with yourself. One way to think about it is to think about how you treat someone you care about. For instance, you could take yourself out to dinner or get a massage or give yourself permission to enjoy the luxury of sleeping in on the weekend.

If you find it challenging to be alone in your own company, consider talking with someone about it. Just like with any relationship, when it gets stuck in an unhelpful place, we can all do with some help to find our way forward. (Check out the "Resources" section at the back of the book for places you can go to for help.)

Daily Check-In

Another way of improving your relationship with yourself is to expand your self-awareness with a daily check-in. This is a way of getting to know yourself better by recognizing and acknowledging what it's like to be you. Making it a regular practice also means that you'll be in a better position to support yourself in the future.

Some people find it helpful to combine a daily check-in with journaling (see page 155), but that's up to you.

**How are you currently feeling
emotionally, mentally, and physically?**

What's been tough today?

What's gone well?

What do you feel grateful for?

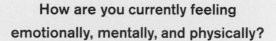

Give the emotions and mental and physical sensations
clear descriptions, and use as many words as you like.
See if you can also accurately detect and name the
underlying emotions. For example, we might describe
ourselves as feeling *upset* or *stressed*, but those umbrella
terms can conceal other important emotional information.
For instance, *stressed* might contain frustration, anger,
helplessness, resentment, sadness, and many more
besides. That said, don't feel you have to stick to
describing your experiences exclusively via the classic
emotions. You might find other language resonates
more for you, like *small*, *vibrant*, or *fizzy*, for example.

Practice Saying No

You might not need any help with this one, in which case feel free to turn the page. But if you're someone who often feels stressed or busy or hassled, this might be for you. Summertime comes with lots of opportunities but that can mean we need to say no sometimes in order to take care of ourselves.

Saying no is a skill and one that we have to learn. If we weren't taught how when we were growing up, then we can be our own teacher now.

It can be helpful to first consider why you keep saying yes. For many of us, it's about not wanting to let people down, wanting people to like us, or being afraid of missing out. Do you think something bad will happen if you say no? Perhaps it's a combination of different things in different situations

and with different people. When you think about the times you say yes when you know you should say no, try to be as honest and as compassionate with yourself as you can.

✳

If you need to, start by saying no to something small. Imagine a low-stress scenario, and act out in your head what you'd like to say and how you'd like to say it. Perhaps consider how you'll stick to it if others try to persuade you. As you walk through the scenario, do any sticking points or barriers come up? How might you coach yourself through them? It might be helpful to write down some of these ideas so you can see them clearly.

✳

Remember, the power of *no* isn't about being negative or denying ourselves things. It's about listening to what feels right for us and not taking unnecessary responsibility for other people.

Drink Water

Not rocket science but harder than it sounds, drinking sufficient water over the course of a day is one of the wellbeing basics. Our energy levels and brain function, such as memory, are impaired when we're dehydrated, and it can cause us to feel more anxious and tired. You'd think that, as it's fundamental to our very survival, we'd have a strong drive to drink enough, but if we haven't developed a regular habit of drinking plenty of water, it can easily go under the radar. Many of us don't even realize when we're dehydrated because we're so accustomed to it.

The common guidance is to aim for about eight glasses (around two liters) a day, but in reality, your fluid needs fluctuate depending on things

like the temperature and exercise. That means you'll probably need more water during the summer. Aim for a level that feels comfortable and sustainable to you. Linking drinking water to your current activities can be a good way of developing a new habit. For instance, you could have a glass when you get up in the morning, before meals, when you get home, while you're watching TV, and after exercise. Even something as simple as carrying a water bottle with you will act as a reminder and make it that much more accessible.

Juices, tea, and coffee all contribute to your fluid intake, but because they also contain sugar or caffeine it's best to set a cap on your consumption. Fizzy and energy drinks full of sugar, caffeine, and additives are worth keeping to a minimum.

More of the Good Stuff

Get a pen and a piece of paper, and cover it with
everything you enjoy. Don't hold back; just get it all
down. Think about what you like to do on your own and
with others, what you enjoy eating, your favorite places,
things you like to do in the morning, in the evening, on the
weekend. Think big and small. What makes you laugh, feel
fulfilled, relaxed—all that good stuff? Write it all down.

Now pick one or two things that you could do in the
next day or week. If you can fit in more, then even better.

Try to pick things that aren't part of your normal routine. For each one you pick, decide a time and schedule it into your diary, as this will make you more likely to do it. Or alternatively, set a reminder on your phone.

Keep the list somewhere you'll see it. You could fix it to the fridge or put it in a frequently used drawer (just don't cover it up).

Keep the list somewhere you'll see it. You could fix it to the fridge or put it in a frequently used drawer (just don't cover it up).

There are times when we all feel like we're on a bit of a treadmill. This activity will connect you with your power to make positive experiences happen. That might be as simple as devoting fifteen minutes of your day to a cup of coffee while people-watching through the cafe window, or as ambitious as organizing a walking tour in Peru. The point is that you chose it, you made the time, and you valued yourself enough to do it.

Dance

Dance classes, music festivals, alone at home with
headphones on and curtains closed—whatever works
for you, see if you can get some dance into your life.
A dance class can be a great way to socialize, and you
can also enjoy the benefits of exercise. But there's
more to dance than just getting to know people and
working out. After all, combining music and movement is
something that binds human societies across the globe
and through the ages, suggesting there is something
about synchronizing your body to a rhythm that is
important and fundamental to being human.
In fact, you could regard the comparative lack of dance
in modern culture as rather odd. A lot of us watch others
doing it, but not so many of us take part. So give your
inner dancer what they've been waiting for—choose
the style, hold the judgment, and take to the floor.

Go Somewhere New

This one can be as adventurous as you want to make it. You can think big and spin the globe to choose a new holiday destination, or you can refresh the everyday by taking a different route home, walking the dog around a different park, or visiting a cafe, museum, or part of town that you've never been to.

♥

When the familiar begins to feel stale, new experiences, no matter how small, can offer a little energy boost as our curiosity engages and our world expands just that little bit more.

Empathy

Empathy is a powerful wellbeing skill to develop. When we practice empathy, we're putting judgment to one side and flexing our curiosity and imagination instead. In order to practice empathy, it's helpful to be clear on the meaning and, importantly, distinguish it from sympathy. Sympathy is when we imagine how a situation that is happening to someone else would affect us. We envision how we would feel and react. The problem is that for sympathy to work as an effective means of understanding others, it would require everyone to be exactly the same.

That's where empathy comes in. It means that we try as best we can to put ourselves in the shoes of another person, to take on their perspective. We consider their worries, their experiences, and their priorities, rather than our own. Empathy can make us a better friend and build closer and stronger relationships while also helping us to act more compassionately towards ourselves.

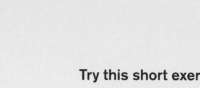

Try this short exercise to start building up your empathy skill.

1. Choose someone you care about, and take a minute or two to think about what it might be like to be them right now.

2. Think about three things they might have been struggling with in the last week.

3. What made you choose each of the three things?

4. Now see if you can come up with three things for which they may have felt grateful today.

5. Again, what made you choose each of the three things?

Community

Feeling connected isn't just about close friends and family; it also involves a broader network of looser connections. This could include colleagues, neighbors, members of groups that you're a part of, shopworkers, delivery people —anyone who adds a thread to the fabric of your social world. They aren't people with whom you necessarily have a great deal in common or in whom you'd confide if you were having a tough time, but they make up your sense of community. And feeling part of a community has been linked to a greater sense of wellbeing.

Depending on your lifestyle, you might have more or fewer of these connections. But whatever point you're starting from, if you feel you could do with more, there are lots of ways to go about it. You could make a start by saying hi to a neighbor or having a quick chat at the till. But one of the best ways to foster a sense of community is to join a community group.

Look out for flyers on noticeboards and local groups on social media. Choose a cause or activity that you're interested in, and see how it goes. You can decide what kind of contact and commitment works for you. Remember, you don't have to make lifelong friends for these relationships to be meaningful and impactful.

Stargazing

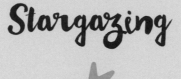

Stargazing is a great summertime activity.
The skies are clearer and the evenings warmer,
making it more likely you'll get a good view and
be comfortable while you're out there.

If you want, you can bring a stargazing guide or app
with you, to help you identify stars, constellations,
galaxies, satellites, and space stations. Alternatively,
you can simply gaze into the sky and sink into the
experience of connecting with the wider universe.

To see the most stars, you'll need a night when the moon
isn't full. That said, the moon itself is worthy of examination,
and you don't need a telescope to do it. A pair of binoculars
can be enough to pick out some of the details on the
moon's surface, including the lighter areas, which indicate
mountains, and darker ones, which indicate lunar seas. The

moon's phases are often misattributed to the earth throwing a shadow across the moon. This does happen during a lunar eclipse, but the regular cycle of the moon's phases is actually caused by its changing position in relation to the sun.

You'll need to give your eyes time to adjust to the dark, so get comfortable with something to sit on and enough layers to keep you warm. The process starts quickly but can take up to thirty minutes to complete. As you're waiting for your eyes to adjust, take a moment to ponder the extraordinary nature of what you're looking at. Light from space travels an astonishing distance before it reaches you. The North Star, for instance, is just over three hundred light years away. This means that when you see it, you're actually looking three hundred years back into the past; that light has taken three hundred years to reach us.

Do Something Nice for Future You

Summertime is great for living in the moment, but casting your mind forward a little can set you up for what's to come. Help support Future You by doing something today that you'll thank yourself for. Here are some ideas to get you started:

◆

Plan a holiday or a break.

Make a big batch of something tasty, and pop it in the freezer so you don't have to think about dinner every night.

Choose and lay out clothes the night before you need them.

Label Tupperware and storage boxes so you know what's inside them.

**Learn to cook something
easy and nutritious.**

Practice that instrument, craft, language, etc.

Go on that walk, run, climb, etc.

**Get that boring/unpleasant
task out of the way.**

◆

When you enjoy the benefits, don't forget to
send appreciation back to Past You.

◆

You can apply this principle to all sorts of decisions.
Just ask yourself, "Will my future self thank me for
this?" That's going to be you in an hour, day, week, or
year. Help them out as best you can in the present.

◆

It's worth adding that sometimes leaving things to Future
You is a helpful choice—for instance, if you're tired and
drained at the end of the day, it's probably best to leave
certain struggles to a time when you have more energy.

Letter of Support

Thinking about doing Future You a favor—why not pre-emptively write yourself a letter of support? This can be particularly helpful if you struggle with anxiety or low mood, or can see that tough times might be ahead.

Think back to when you've struggled in the past. What do you wish you could have known then? What did you learn from those experiences? How did you help yourself through? What resources did you tap into? What did you lose sight of that you want to keep close next time?

Write it as you would a letter. You know yourself better than anyone, so you know how best to put it and what you'll be most likely to listen to. So avoid hollow platitudes and use language that resonates.

When you're finished, pop it in your self-care toolbox (see page 120), so it's there when it's needed.

Slow Down

Autumn is the perfect season for trying out a slower tempo. Start small by doing one thing today at a slower pace than usual. Here are some ideas to get you started, but you can always devise your own.

Eat a meal more slowly, and savor the tastes and textures.

Go for a stroll rather than a walk.

Take a few minutes to breathe slowly and deeply.

Sit and listen to music rather than treating it as background noise (see page 26).

Slow the pace down on your
nighttime routine.

Look at a piece of art (or a pet
playing or the clouds passing
overhead, etc.) for five minutes.

Call someone rather than text.

Put your phone away for an evening
(turn to "Digital Detox for a Day" on page
106 if you want to take this further).

Wake up fifteen minutes earlier than usual,
and have a more leisurely breakfast.

Say no to something (see page 68).

Enjoy being present in silence for a few minutes.

Grounding

Grounding is when we consciously reconnect our minds and bodies to the present moment. When we're in an anxious state, we often find our thoughts spinning up into worries about the future or regrets about the past. Grounding techniques are designed to bring you back to the present moment, reminding you of the stability and safety of the here and now.

You can do this particular mindfulness-based exercise practically anywhere, and it's easy to remember with the "Five, Four, Three, Two, One" formula. And don't worry if you mix them up and find yourself naming five things you can hear and four things you can touch; the point is to reconnect with the present through your senses in whatever order works for you.

Name:

Five things you can see

Four things you can hear

Three things you can touch

Two things you can smell

One thing you can taste

Feel free to move around to find things to name, but do, in the first instance, check your immediate surroundings. As well as naming each thing, don't forget to connect with your senses as you go.

Connect with Wildlife

We know that being in nature is good for our mental health, and that includes observing wildlife. The good news is that even the most urban environments can be home to a variety of species. Parks are welcome havens for wildlife, and you might be surprised by the diversity on offer in yours. If you can, explore a local wood or riverbank, or find out if there are any nature reserves in your area.

Binoculars can add to the experience, giving you a close-up view of animals and birds that would normally avoid humans, and revealing fascinating details of appearance

and behavior. But even just spotting them with
the naked eye can make for a memorable encounter.

If you have some outdoor space, can you make it
more welcoming to wildlife? You could set up bird
feeders and bug hotels, and think about what would make
your garden more amenable to whatever wild mammals
live in your neighborhood. One of the biggest impacts you
can have on the level of diversity in your garden is to add
a pond. And it needn't be large. Even a sink-sized pond
can be home to a range of amphibians and invertebrates,
and it will provide drinking water for visiting mammals and
birds. You could also alter your gardening style, such as
avoiding pesticides and herbicides, leaving grass to grow
longer during the summer, and allowing a patch to run
completely wild. All of this will provide food and habitat
for insects and animals, while giving you a front-row seat.

Acts of Kindness

Over the next week, aim to commit to one act of kindness every day. Think about the people in your life to whom you would like to show kindness and what they might appreciate. It doesn't have to be a grand gesture—although it certainly can be if inspiration strikes—because kindness can be felt in even the small gestures, such as offering to cook dinner or handling a chore that you don't normally do. It might be taking the time to ask someone how they're doing and really listening to the answer. Or it might be telling a loved one just how much they mean to you.

One approach is to plan out your acts of kindness
in advance. That way they can be tailor-made,
and you're also less likely to forget to do them.
Alternatively, you could look out for spontaneous
opportunities, such as helping a stranger with
their luggage up some stairs, giving up your seat
on the bus or train, donating books and clothes to
charity, or buying a coffee for someone in need.

See how it goes and pay attention to how
it feels. Being kind to others can be a real
win-win in terms of wellbeing as it leaves the
giver and the recipient feeling good.

Cold-Water Therapy

Cold-water therapy essentially involves immersing ourselves in cold water—around 60°F is low enough— even just briefly for the physical and mental benefits. People have been doing this for centuries all over the globe, but it's recently had a revival. Among other health advantages, cold-water therapy is reported to improve sleep and energy levels, and some people have found it has helped with symptoms of low mood and anxiety.

The easiest way of trying it for yourself is with cold showers. But that doesn't mean you should just jump straight in—it'll likely be so unpleasant you'll never do it again! The best approach is to take it slowly and build up your resilience over time. So at the end of your usual warm shower, drop the temperature a bit for about half a minute. With each subsequent shower, your aim is to reduce the temperature that bit more and stand there for longer. Your end goal is five minutes with the water running fully cold.

If you're feeling adventurous, you could try wild swimming. Swimmer-friendly lakes, rivers, unheated outdoor pools, and the sea are all excellent options. If you're a novice, take someone with you, as it can take some getting used to, and make sure to ease yourself in slowly. As with cold showers, you don't have to be in the water for long. A few minutes will suffice. Make sure you warm up thoroughly when you get out. That means drying off, putting on layers of warm clothes, and having a warm drink and something to eat—the sugars help bring up your body temperature.

Be aware that this is not for everyone! Especially if you have any health concerns where the shock of cold water might pose a risk. Consult your doctor if you're unsure, don't start in the middle of winter if you've never done it before, and only swim where you are sure it's safe.

The Power of Laughter

We make time for lots of things we recognize as important —work, family, exercise—so why not laughter? Laughter is a wonderful natural antidote to stress. It reduces physical tension, triggers the release of endorphins, strengthens social bonds, and can help you shift to a more positive frame of mind. But you probably know all of this instinctively anyway.

✻

How might you bring more laughter into your life? Are there comedies that you enjoy watching on screen? YouTube channels? Books? Cartoon strips? How about stand-up comics? We're far more likely to laugh when we're with others, so it's worth thinking about those in your life who make you laugh and whether you might like to see them a little more.

Letting Go

As autumn comes around, trees prepare by breaking
down and reabsorbing chlorophyll, the green pigment
in their leaves. Over summer, they were busy converting
sunlight into energy, but now they're no longer needed.
The tree drops its leaves, as to hold on to them would
mean expending valuable energy on maintaining things
that are no longer nourishing it. By letting the leaves go,
the tree is able to preserve resources and better tolerate
winter storms, as strong winds can move through the
branches more easily. This ensures that come spring,
the tree is in good shape to burst into life once more.

❋

Do you have any leaves that you'd like to drop in order
to move into your own spring? For the tree, it is a process
of withdrawing energy and allowing the leaves to fall.
If you feel that you could do with some help working
through this process (we're a bit more complicated
than trees, after all), turn to the "Resources" section
at the back of this book for sources of support.

Make Something

...anything. If you're someone who mainly
uses their hands to tap a keyboard, this
one might be just what you need.

Our minds and fingers have evolved to be incredibly
skillful. It's one of the reasons why we've been so
remarkably successful as a species. That drive to craft
tools, clothes, machinery, cookware, and generally
turn our hands to creating and constructing has meant
we've adapted, evolved, and thrived. And there seems
to be a connection between this drive and a feeling

of wellbeing. Many craftspeople report a sense of satisfaction and rightness when they use their hands.

If making things is no longer a part of your job or daily experience, consider whether you'd like to take up a new practical or creative hobby. After all, the breadth of options is vast. Be it a model airplane, ceramic pot, knitted scarf, giant Lego monolith…there's likely something you'll enjoy creating. To try out different skills, use online videos, consult instruction manuals, join classes, or just experiment freestyle. When you start, remember to keep your expectations realistic. Beginners do not create expert outcomes, so the pressure's off. At first, try to focus on the process, not the product. If you like doing it, then you know it's worth investing more time to improve your skill.

Magnify

On your next walk in nature gather up a few
finds: small pebbles, feathers, seed heads,
nut cases, buds, and leaves that have fallen
from plants are all good candidates

When you get home (or while you're out if you don't
mind bringing the magnifying glass with you), lay them
out in front of you. Select one object and examine it.

First with the naked eye, take in its outline, the colors, the texture, the scent. Then use your magnifying glass to look closer. Take your time observing the level of detail it reveals. There will be new colors and new textures to appreciate. The magnification provides a new perspective and shows us elements that were outside our awareness before.

Feathers can be especially rewarding, as the magnifying glass reveals the extraordinary engineering involved in their construction. Even the most dull-looking feather will, in reality, exhibit an exquisite pattern of interlocking shades and shapes. Even the humble pebble has far more to it than our natural level of vision allows us to appreciate.

Gratitude Diary

Practicing gratitude can have a meaningful impact on our sense of wellbeing. It can realign our view away from what we feel we lack or want, to what we already have in the here and now. Crucially, gratitude isn't about denying the tough parts of life or suppressing sad, angry, or uncomfortable feelings. Rather, it's about making sure that we aren't overlooking the good stuff when it's there. Gratitude may help us to recognize overlooked sources of positivity while getting better connected to what really matters to us. The benefits can include boosted mood, lower anxiety and stress levels, and a more positive view of the world and yourself.

To get the greatest benefit, it helps to develop a regular practice. Just before bed can be a good time as you look back over your day. You can practice gratitude in your head, but keeping a physical diary may be more effective, as it slows down the process, encourages you to formulate your thoughts clearly, and makes it easier to reflect. It can also be interesting to look back on months later.

The practice itself is as simple as noting down three things for which you felt grateful for today. They may be the simplest of things. Try to keep it varied so you aren't just coming back to the same things. Be sure to give yourself time to really experience the emotional sensation of gratitude. For example, you could consider what it is precisely about that thing that made you feel grateful. Keep a notebook next to your bed with a pen or pencil ready as a reminder. Try it every day for a couple of weeks, and see how it feels.

Digital Detox for a Day

Do you think you could go a whole day without your phone? If this sounds like a breeze, then feel free to turn the page. But if you found your pulse quicken at the very idea, then you might find this a helpful experiment.

To be clear, there's nothing wrong with phones, and you might be perfectly comfortable with how you use yours. But for some of us, being accessible twenty-four hours a day, distracted by intrusive notifications, and tempted by the siren call of various social media platforms can be unhelpful and unwelcome. It's also not always obvious how our devices are impacting us—taking a break can help bring that to light. We can then use the information to make conscious choices about how we use our devices (see "Digital Spring-Clean" on page 17 for more ideas on this).

One way is to simply put your phone away for one whole day. You can choose the day so it causes you minimal disruption, and if you think there are people who may worry about your lack of response, then give them a heads-up beforehand. Ideally, put your phone out of sight so it doesn't lure you back.

If a whole day isn't possible, try half a day. Or you could start with an hour or two, and then build up. If circumstances mean you can't be without a phone, or it makes you feel uncomfortable, keep it with you but turned off. You could schedule particular times in the day when you check your phone, respond to anything urgent, and then put it away again.

Remember to give yourself time to reflect on the experience. What feelings did it stir up? Perhaps it was stressful and/ or a relief to be without a phone? How did it affect your day? What did you do more or less of? What does the experience tell you about your relationship with your device? Would you like to make any changes?

You could even take it a step further with a no-screen day—that's no phones, no computers, no TV...no looking at a screen for a whole day.

Go for a Walk in the Rain

On the whole, we try to avoid the rain. We cover up
with raincoats and umbrellas if we have to, preferring to
retreat indoors and watch it balefully through the window.
But what if, just for once, we were to fully embrace it?

Choose a day that has some proper rain—something with
a bit of oomph to it—and make sure you're wearing clothes
that you don't mind getting wet. Leave as much as you
can behind—your phone might not enjoy the experience.

Brisk walking will help you to keep warm, but don't forget
to stop occasionally. When you pause, close your eyes
and turn your face to the sky. Give yourself time to feel the
raindrops on your face and to hear the sound of them as
they hit the various surfaces around you. Smell the change
they make to the air. Open your mouth to

let the drops fall on your tongue. What words would you use to describe the taste? The good news is that rainy days tend to mean fewer people, so you're less likely to be disturbed—and will perhaps be less self-conscious!

Once you've enjoyed the full sensory experience that rain has to offer (don't stay out longer than is comfortable —just a few minutes can be enough) and have started back home, you could ponder the remarkable properties of rain. For example, the average raindrop travels more than two miles from its cloud to the earth, its journey taking around two or three minutes. Each molecule of H_2O inside it has been on an extraordinary journey before it reaches the cloud: across oceans, down mountains, through the internal structures of plants and trees. You could even contemplate where it will go in the future.

Once you get home, your top priority is getting dry and warm. You might like to take a shower to heat up or just pop on some cozy clothes. After the invigoration of the rain, there's nothing better than relaxing in the warmth afterwards.

Release the Thoughts

The next time whirring thoughts or worries are causing your stress or anxiety levels to rise, see if this technique helps take some of the pressure off.

Get yourself a piece of paper and a pen, and start writing about how you're feeling and thinking. Don't worry about the writing itself; just let the words flow. Spelling, grammar, style, fluency are all irrelevant here. Cover the page if you need to, and if one page isn't enough, get another and keep going. Studies have shown that the more words you use, the more anxiety and stress levels drop, so don't hold back.

There's no need to read back over what you're writing or make any judgments about yourself as you go. This exercise is all about the process of expression, of allowing all those thoughts a release, out of your head and onto the page.

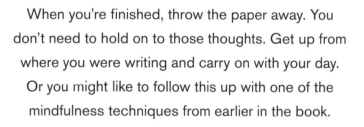

When you're finished, throw the paper away. You don't need to hold on to those thoughts. Get up from where you were writing and carry on with your day. Or you might like to follow this up with one of the mindfulness techniques from earlier in the book.

Improve Your Environment

As autumn hits we tend to spend more time inside. Where do you spend most of your day? Perhaps it's at a desk in an office, in your kitchen, or at the wheel of your car. Right now, have a think about what one thing you could do to make that space more pleasant to be in. It might be adding a reed diffuser or candle, installing a supportive cushion for your back, hanging a picture, personalizing the space with a photograph that makes you smile, arranging some flowers in a vase, or something quite different.

Of course, you needn't stop at just one thing. Feel free to let your imagination loose; you might consider the color of the walls, the arrangement of the space (turn back to "Refresh a Room" on page 42 for more ideas), or the level of light. But remember, it doesn't have to be complicated to make a difference. The purpose here is not only to improve your everyday environment; it's also a way of showing yourself that you are of value and worthy of the effort to make things that bit nicer for you.

Storytelling

These days, we tend to see story time as something exclusively to be enjoyed by children, but in times past and still today in certain cultures around the world, storytelling has a rich and varied role in society as entertainment, community bonding, delivering news, and recording historical events.

There is much joy to be had in simply telling and listening to stories, and there are many ways you can go about it. You could read aloud from a book—short stories can be a great option to begin with. But there is also something satisfying in the episodic nature of working your way through a whole novel over the course of a month or so. You could also make up your own stories or even recount plotlines from films that you've seen—feel free to embellish as you go; it's the storyteller's prerogative. If you aren't able to get together in person, storytelling can work just as well over video calls or the phone, or you could even record yourself telling a story and send it to a friend. But if you don't want to involve others, why not try an audiobook; sample something a bit different, or go to an old favorite, and enjoy the narrator doing all the different voices.

Get Good at Failure

Sometimes things don't work out. In fact, it's not possible to go through life without experiencing failures and disappointments. They are a part of living, and though we try to influence outcomes, we are never wholly in control of them. What we do have a say over is how we respond to them when they happen.

Ask yourself right now, how do you react to disappointment and failure? How do you treat yourself after it happens? What do you imagine it means about you that things didn't go to plan?

Now imagine someone else is telling you a story of having experienced the same thing. How would you treat them? What would you say? What would you think it meant about them?

Is there a difference between how you respond to yourself and somebody else? We may offer others more understanding and compassion than we offer ourselves. Which approach do you think is the most helpful? Can you shift your approach to yourself to be more encouraging? How might you do that?

Collect Color

Autumn is a beautiful season. Summer might be celebrated for its bold and vibrant rainbow splashes, but with autumn comes a softer, more sophisticated palette of ombrés. Browns and oranges come into their own, with warm ochers and golden yellows, bronzed russets and honeyed tans.

On your next walk, gather specimens for an autumnal showcase by collecting nature finds as you go. Look for fallen leaves, feathers, acorns, seed cases, and twigs. Only take what's already fallen to avoid causing damage. When you get home, lay your finds out in front of you, then arrange them by color into a pleasing spectrum.

This kind of art is temporary by nature, so take a picture when you're finished if you want to remember it in the future. Alternatively, you can embrace the spirit of autumn and allow your creation to be of the moment. When you've finished appreciating the beauty, return your finds outside where they will rejoin the local ecosystem, providing nutrition and habitat for local plants and wildlife.

Self-Care Toolbox

You might have already come across the idea of a self-care toolbox. It's where you collect together items that you find reassuring and encouraging so that they're ready and available for tough times. You can use any old box as long as it's big enough to contain a few of the key items, but you might like to decorate it or get a box that feels a bit more special.

What might you include? It could be a pair of fluffy socks, photos of loved ones, postcards or letters that make you smile, your favorite book—this book! Add lists of other things that make you feel good, such as favorite films or TV episodes, comfort foods, or activities you like. A list of names and numbers of people who you can turn to when you need to talk can be a useful addition. It's also a great place to keep that letter of support you wrote from earlier in the book (see page 85).

How's It Going?

As you've been working your way through the book, have you found any of the activities particularly tough or challenging?

What was difficult about them?

Have you learned anything about yourself from the experience?

Is there anything that you would like to change or do differently going forward?

How could you support yourself to make those changes?

Are there any other questions that feel important?

How might you explore them further?

Sunsets

Winter is one of the best times of year to watch sunsets. It's when the colors appear at their most intense and the sunset is most drawn out. They also happen earlier in the day, so you're more likely to catch them. And finally, in a season that can otherwise feel gray and drained of color, they make for a glorious feast for the eyes.

Give them the time and attention they deserve. When you notice one (these things can't always be planned), see if you can pause, slow down, and just take it in. Knowing that you're watching the action of the earth turning beneath your feet and that the light that's hitting your eye has travelled about 93 million miles just to get to you can be a truly awe-inspiring and mind-stilling experience.

Take Up More Space

Try this exercise to see what taking up more space feels like. This isn't about posture as such; it's more about giving yourself permission to take up all the space you need and not collapsing in on yourself, as is so easy when we're tired or anxious.

❊

Sit or lie in a comfortable position.

Imagine a line running from the top of your head down to the bottom of your spine.

Now imagine that line lengthening.

Next, imagine another line running from one shoulder to the other, across your body.

Imagine that line lengthening also.

If you're sitting down, gently straighten your
back to lift your chest away from your middle,
expanding the space inside your torso.

Inhale deeply, filling your lungs.

Notice how your ribs and muscles
expand outward in all directions.

Pen Pal

Emails, texts, calls, messages, posts, tweets…
we have never had so many ways to communicate
with one another, and with such extraordinary
ease. Given that feeling connected directly
impacts our sense of wellbeing, this is all for
the good. But with an increase in quantity, we
can lose out on quality. Though they may feel
antiquated, that's where letters win hands down.

A letter communicates not just what's written,
but also the time and care that was taken in the
writing. Handwriting displays personal qualities
that are lost in digital mediums. A letter also insists
on a change of pace. A letter must be written,
posted, delivered, and read. A quiet focus comes
when we write with a pen in hand; we can be
expressive, and we can illustrate our points with
flourishes, ornamentation, and even drawings.

Then, once our letter is written, there is a pleasurable pause as we wait for a reply. The reading of a letter can also be more deliberate. We may sit down with intention, perhaps accompanied by a warming cup of something as we honor the letter writer's time and care with our own. Unlike digital communications, which usually exist only on screens, letters can be held and treasured—they also make great additions to a self-care toolbox (see page 120).

♥

If you would like to have a go at letter writing but aren't sure where to start, many charities run letter-writing projects for the elderly, refugees, those struggling with mental health, and many others, and are always grateful for volunteers.

Nesting

Is there a space in your home where you could create a small sanctuary? Somewhere you can retreat to and feel comfortable and relaxed, it might be a room, a particular chair or corner of the sofa, or even your bed. It doesn't need to be a permanent spot if that isn't possible, just one that you can turn into a space to relax when you need it. It's a perfect place for that quality me-time we discussed back in "Soothing Solitude"(page 64)— somewhere you can read a book, listen to music, watch a film, gaze out of the window, or simply doze off.

Once you've decided on that spot, you can begin the 'nesting' process, making the space special and inviting. Start by giving the area a good clean so you have a blank canvas to work from. Then furnish it. You could install some cozy cushions, a blanket, and perhaps a plant or scented candle, whatever you feel would enhance the space. Think about lighting. A small table light or even a string of fairy lights can help demarcate the area and make it feel more welcoming.

Don't worry if none of these ideas appeal—this is your nest, and you can decorate it however you like.

Box Breathing

This is a great breathing exercise for any time you want to dial down anxiety or stress. It only takes a few minutes, and once you've got the hang of it, you can use it practically anywhere.

It's called 'box breathing' because, as you're regulating your breathing, you're also following the outline of a square with your eyes. You don't have to use the square, but it can help to keep you fully focused.

1. Sit in a comfortable position with your feet flat on the floor and your back relaxed but straight.

2. Locate a square shape in front of you. It could be a windowpane, a picture frame, or you could use the picture of a square provided on the next page.

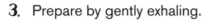

3. Prepare by gently exhaling.

4. Now, inhale through your nose to a slow count of four. As you breathe in, follow one side of the square with your eyes.

5. Hold that breath for another count of four as you run your eyes along the next side of the square.

6. Exhale through your mouth to a slow count of four while moving your eyes along the third side of the square.

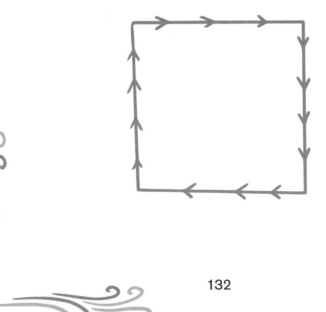

7. Pause and hold for another count of four as you run your eyes along the last side of the square.

Try just one or two cycles at first, and then build up to about four as you feel more confident. If you find yourself getting light-headed or rushing, then speed up your counting. Aim for a comfortable, manageable experience.

Rest

Most of us are aware that good-quality sleep aids wellbeing, but rest is different from sleep. Rest is something that we do during the day to relax and recharge. It is inherently low-energy and restorative. It can feel a bit novel these days, as the concept of rest isn't prized in modern society, with the consequence that we feel more stressed and lacking in time.

There are many ways we can take rest. It might be a few minutes with a glass of something refreshing or a weeklong holiday; it could be a lazy day or a half-hour's daydreaming. But the key is that we do *take* it.

How do you rest? Do you rest? How might you work in periods of rest to your coming week? Set times and boundaries so they become commitments. It can also help to consciously transition into your period of rest by changing environment, such as moving rooms or just seats. To ease your body into a lower-energy mode, why not start with a minute or two of a simple breathing exercise, such as "Box Breathing" on page 131?

★

Give your rest an end point and stick to it.
If you know that resting doesn't disrupt but rather enhances the rest of your day, you're more likely to actually do it.

Plan Something Fun

When was the last time you did something just because it was fun? We're not talking activities that are productive or purposeful—although they may be these things as well—but rather those things you do just because they give you that light hearted, playful feeling.

We expect children to play; in fact, we see how important it is for them to do so. But as we grow

into adulthood, the focus shifts to responsibilities and achievements. Fun and play get overlooked, and we find that things we used to enjoy doing slip away without us noticing. We're left with a lot more seriousness and a lot less levity. But what if you were to redress the balance?

Write a list of activities that you find fun. Think about what you found fun in the past as well as more recently. Consider things that you might like to try in the future. The next part is to actually do them. Planning ahead might not sound super fun and spontaneous, but it can be a really effective way of making changes. Get a date in the planner, stick to it, and see what difference it makes.

Give Back

As with "Acts of Kindness" on page 94, giving back is a
win-win for wellbeing. It can help us to feel connected
and positive about the world and our place within it.

Tree planting, litter picking, offering hospital transport, giving
blood, volunteering at a helpline—there are so many options.
Choose an area that you care about and see what's out there.
There are all sorts of organizations that are deeply grateful for
offers of help. It could be a regular commitment or a one-off.
There can be a social element to it if you like, or not. Find the fit
for you and see what it's like. Local noticeboards and groups on
social media are good places to start looking for opportunities.

If you're feeling more ambitious and you have an
idea for what you'd like to do, but there isn't already
a group up and running that you could join, you
could always think about setting it up yourself.

Bake Yourself
a Cookie

Sometimes we could all do with a cookie. And baking can be a wonderfully mindful process if you want it to be, as each step engages your senses in a different way. Watch the colors and consistencies of the ingredients combine as you mix, feel the texture of the dough as you form the cookie shapes, inhale the aroma as they rise in the oven, and then, finally, enjoy that blissful experience of tasting a warm, just-out-of-the-oven cookie.

The recipe below is for a classic chocolate chip cookie, but feel free to adapt it to your own tastes.

Ingredients:

1 cup sugar (whatever mixture of brown and white you like)

3/4 cup softened butter (dairy or nondairy)

1 egg (or egg alternative, such as 1 tbsp ground flax seed mixed with 3 tbsps of water)

2 1/2 cups self-rising flour

1 1/2 cups milk or dark chocolate (broken into small chunks)

Method:

1. Preheat your oven to 350°F.

2. Add the sugar and softened butter to a bowl and mix.

3. Add the egg and combine until the color appears paler.

4. Add the flour and chocolate and mix again.

5. Separate the mixture into balls, approximately the size of golf balls.

6. Line a baking tray with baking parchment, place the balls on top, and then flatten with the palm of your hand until they're approximately half an inch thick.

7. Pop them in the oven for eight minutes. When they come out, they'll still be slightly gooey.

8. Leave them to cool before digging in.

Stretch

As it gets colder, our focus switches to staying warm, dry, and cozy, and if our daily lives involves sitting down for long stretches, then come winter, that can mean we're even more sedentary than usual.

As a result, we may miss out on opportunities to release tension and stress that's built up within our bodies. Our emotions play out within our body as well as our minds, which is why movement is one way to process our feelings and experiences. It's why some people find a regular walk, yoga, or exercise helpful in restoring a sense of emotional balance.

Some of us can store our feelings of worry or upset as tension in particular places in our bodies. You might already know where you keep yours. Look out for areas of tightness and stiffness. Or you could try a body scan to find out (see page 60). Common areas for holding stress are the jaw, neck, and shoulders.

Regularly getting up and moving around, taking walks, and frequent exercise are all great ways to get the muscles moving and flexible again, but you can also stretch out particular problem areas. Remember to stretch slowly and carefully—just enough to feel the pull is sufficient. If you're in pain, stop. Overstretching can cause damage.

❋

Try this simple neck stretching exercise to get started.

1. Stand or sit up straight.

2. Take a few slow, deep breaths to help relax your body.

3. Start with your head in a forward-facing, level position.

4. Lower your chin towards your chest and hold for twenty seconds, then slowly lift your head back to level.

5. Raise your chin towards the ceiling and hold for about ten seconds. Return your head to a level position.

6. Gently tilt your head to the side and towards your right shoulder, as if you're trying to bring your ear closer to your shoulder. Hold it for about ten seconds. Then return your head to level.

7. Repeat on your left side.

8. Turn your head to the right as if you are looking over your right shoulder. Hold the stretch for about twenty seconds.

9. Repeat on your left side.

10. You can now repeat the whole exercise a few more times, as many as feels comfortable.

Animals

If you've got animals in your life, you're probably already
aware of their effect on your sense of wellbeing.
But for those without, they can be worth seeking
out, whether that's seeing a friend with pets, visiting
a community farm, volunteering for a dog-walking
business, or donating your time to an animal rescue.

Spending time with animals can take us out of
ourselves—our worries and hang-ups mean nothing to
them. They have their own priorities and are great at
demonstrating what living in the present truly looks like.

And if domesticated animals aren't your thing, what
about something a bit wilder (see page 92)?

Devise Your Own Recipe

This is a great activity for the winter months, when the kitchen offers a welcome source of warmth, light, and coziness. And don't worry about your culinary prowess; you don't need to be a gastronomic master to make your own recipe. The purpose here is to exercise a bit of creativity in an area where some of us can find ourselves doing the same old thing or relying on recipe books. That said, even if you are a great experimenter in the kitchen, if you haven't already got a dish that bears your name, then there's still something here for you.

The first step is to choose your medium: Do you want to devise a whole meal or just a single element? Is cooking or baking more your thing? Then consider how original you'd like to be. For instance, you could craft your recipe from scratch, or take an old classic and add a twist that makes it personal to you. Think about the kinds of food you love—the flavors, the textures, dishes you grew up with or discovered later in life. Or perhaps you've actually already got a signature dish that just wants naming.

Once you have your recipe, it's up to you what you do with it. You could use it as an excuse to have friends or family around to eat together or make up recipe cards to give as gifts. Or perhaps you'd like to keep the secret of your recipe to yourself and enjoy it as part of your quality me-time.

Luxuriate in the Little Things

Depending on how you use it, mindfulness can make for a wonderfully luxurious experience. When we luxuriate in a bubble bath, for instance, we're embracing the experience fully through our senses, sinking into the soothing warmth, and enjoying the delicious fragrances. A mindful experience if ever there was one!

✳

You can bring this luxuriating, mindful approach to even everyday habits. One such way is to take your time while washing your hands to inhale the scent of the soap and feel the silkiness of the suds. Or how about in the shower, with shower gel and shampoo? Moisturizing is another good opportunity to elevate the experience by focusing on the sensation of applying the moisturizer, watching as it sinks in, and appreciating how it's nourishing your skin. You probably took care choosing the products that you use, so why not reap the benefits? Nighttime

routines are a perfect time for luxuriating in these little things. You're already slowing down, and by taking a mindful approach, you can make the process a really calming and restorative one.

You can apply the same principle to the food and drink you consume. Challenge yourself to pause before you start eating or drinking, and remind yourself to really taste that first sip or first bite. Or what about the clothes you wear? You've probably chosen those super cozy socks or a soft sweater for a reason. Fresh bed linens are another one of those routine joys that shouldn't be wasted.

Are there any other routine things that could be better enjoyed with a dose of mindfulness?

Feel-Good Entertainment

This could be one to combine with the "Self-Care Toolbox" on page 120. It's where you create a list of things that make you feel good, which you can turn to for inspiration when times get tough.

This is a bit different from a list of things you enjoy. Those are important too, of course, but not all of the things we enjoy always make us feel good. For instance, you might love true-crime podcasts, but they might also leave you feeling slightly on edge. This list is about pulling together the things that you do that help you to feel safe, secure, and optimistic. Think about films, TV, books, sports, music, poetry, art, crafts—anything you do for entertainment that you find helpful and soothing.

One way to go about it is to get a pen and a piece of paper, and then cover it with ideas—no filter and no editing. Just get it all down. Once you've got the raw material in front of you, sort through each idea, assessing how it makes you feel when you do it. If it fits the bill, then you can include it in your final feel-good list.

★

Once you've finished the list, keep it somewhere accessible so it's handy when you're struggling. It's an ideal addition to your self-care toolbox, but you don't have to keep it in one place. For example, you could take a picture on your phone so it's always close by. And don't forget to keep adding to it.

Sunshine

The benefits of vitamin D are pretty well known these days. It's involved in maintaining bone, muscle, and dental health, supporting your immune system, and regulating blood pressure, among other health advantages. You can obtain vitamin D from your diet, but sunshine is another important source—your body actually creates vitamin D when sunlight hits your skin.

Sunshine not only supports your physical health; it has other properties that bestow extra benefits, which include promoting better sleep, a sense of wellbeing, and improved mood. This can be especially important in the wintertime, when we're exposed to less sunshine. Some people can experience SAD (seasonal affective disorder), where lack of sunshine causes temporary depression.

If you're someone who spends a lot of time indoors, a daily walk can make a world of difference. You'll also get the added boost of some gentle exercise. And don't worry if it's overcast; while the intensity of UVB rays is lessened by cloud cover, enough will still likely be getting through to make it worth it. If you're not able to get outside, try sitting by an open window in a sunny spot for ten minutes—it has to be open, because glass filters out the UVB rays, which your body needs to make the vitamin D.

Depending on where you live, you may still need to take care to limit sun exposure to a safe level even in winter, and use protection such as sunscreen, cover-ups, and hats when necessary.

Start a Journal

Many people find journaling to be a powerful wellbeing tool. It's a way to check in with our feelings and experiences, and offers us a place to process them, externalizing what's going on inside. By getting our thoughts and emotions down on the page, we create distance, often bringing us clarity or a different perspective. We can choose to reflect on what we write or simply close the page and leave it there.

There's no one way to journal either. Some people like pen and paper, and others prefer a digital format. Some develop a daily routine, whereas for others it's more sporadic. And if words aren't your medium, then try illustration or color, or attach mementos. Remember, this is your journal; no one else is going to see it, so what you choose to journal about and how you do it is entirely up to you.

The Familiar

There are times for trying new things and venturing out into the unknown, and then there are times when we need the soothing balm of the familiar. Being able to return to that reassuring security of the known is especially important during periods of change and uncertainty. The familiar can act as an anchor that helps us to endure the buffeting of life's challenges.

★

The refuge of the familiar can be found in all sorts of places—in books, photos, clothes, places, routines, or rituals. It might be the Christmas movies that you watch every year, or the regularity and constancy of Sunday lunch. It might be settling down to watch your favorite period drama or wrapping up in an old and beloved hoodie. Where do you find that soothing familiarity in your life? Add a few of these to your self-care toolbox (see page 120), or write them on your self-care list, so you have them when you need them.

Look Out for New Life

For many of us, winter feels like a long slog. Lower light levels, dreary weather, colder temperatures, and a landscape drained of color can all contribute to a decline in mood and reduced energy levels. We find ourselves longing for the new life, light, and color of spring.

The good news is that you can start looking for signs of spring even while winter appears to be in full swing. Keep your eyes sharp for green shoots pushing their way out of the soil, as well as buds forming on bushes and trees; remember that things can change in a matter of days, so keep checking.

And don't forget to mark the lengthening of the days. Once the winter solstice has passed, light levels are actually increasing every day, even as temperatures drop. Furthermore, despite the appearance of a hibernating landscape, there is still much that flourishes during even the coldest months, whether that's evergreen trees, winter-flowering plants, or birds that visit over winter. And if you're in need of more color, check out "Sunsets" on page 124.

Resources

SAMARITANS USA

For anyone who is struggling, feels overwhelmed or needs a listening ear, 24 hours a day, 365 days a year, visit www.samaritansusa.org.

MIND

National Institute of Mental Health Provides advice and support via their website www.nimh.gov.

Primary Care Physician

If you need further support, your primary care physician is a great place to start. They will help guide you towards a range of resources and make decisions about what might be best for you.

If you are in crisis, don't hesitate to reach out. You can phone 911 or go straight to the ER for immediate help.